CHIEFS OF THE SEA AND SKY

CHIEFS OF T

HE SEA AND SKY

Haida Heritage Sites of the Queen Charlotte Islands

George F. MacDonald

Publication of this book has been made possible in part by a grant from
Dr. Margaret P. Hess

University of British Columbia Press
Vancouver 1989

© THE UNIVERSITY OF BRITISH COLUMBIA PRESS 1989
All rights reserved
ISBN 0-7748-0331-2

This book has been abridged from *Haida Monumental Art:
Villages of the Queen Charlotte Islands*
·by George F. MacDonald
(Vancouver: University of British Columbia Press 1983)

Canadian Cataloguing in Publication Data
MacDonald, George F.
Chiefs of the Sea and Sky

Abridged version of: Haida Monumental Art
Bibliography: p.
ISBN 0-7748-0331-2

1. Haida Indians — Art.   2. Haida Indians — Sculpture.
3. Haida Indians — Architecture.   4. Indians of North
America — British Columbia — Queen Charlotte Islands
— Art.   5. Indians of North America — British Columbia
— Queen Charlotte Islands — Sculpture.   6. Indians of
North America — British Columbia — Queen Charlotte
Islands — Architecture.   I. Title.
E99.H2M32 1989   704'.0397   C89-091171-1

Designed by Robin Ward
Typeset by The Typeworks, Vancouver
Printed in Canada by Hignell Printing, Winnipeg

CONTENTS

FOREWORD

SOME DAY SOON I HOPE the native people of the North-west Coast and members of the strange tribe who inhabit the groves of Academe will overcome the last of the mistrust and suspicion which have always lurked, some-times hidden, sometimes overt, in their long relation-ship, and realize how truly symbiotic it has been. Of course, the academics have always been totally depen-dent on the raw stuff of native culture to feed their word machines, but only recently have some of the native peoples begun to realize, as the older generations pass from the scene taking their verbal recollections ir-revocably with them, how dependent they have become on the words and pictures of the academic community for knowledge of their histories and almost forgotten cul-tural achievements.

This remarkable volume, assembled over the past two decades by George MacDonald, should provide a strong support for the bridge between the two groups, as well as an eye-opening revelation for the wider community. It is concerned entirely with the Haidas of the Queen Char-lotte Islands of the last century, the intricacies of the kinship patterns of the great families, and how they saw themselves as part of a fantastic, but in its own terms logical, cosmos, and most of all how this was all ex-pressed in their remarkable architecture with its per-fectly integrated, massive, carved and painted embellish-ments, the great totem poles of the Haidas.

Today, where the villages exemplifying this style of life once stood, there are in the two remaining inhabited communities only clusters of sometimes neat and well-built, sometimes run down and untidy, uninteresting little conventional cottages and the inevitable mobile homes. In the long-abandoned sites, a few corpses of decayed wood which were proud poles and massive house beams lie on or under mossy blankets, soon to be crushed completely by the slow march of the returning forest.

These would become mere memories of memories, images as faint as Atlantis, as remote from us as the lives of those who built and lived in them.

But there were those inspired, dedicated, stubborn, persistent eccentrics who painfully lugged the enormous, cumbersome, glorious pieces of equipment that were the early cameras to these still remote shores, set them up, and recorded what they saw so fully and accurately that today a skilled interpreter, Dr. MacDonald in this in-stance, can reconstruct not only the physical façade of those distant times but also, adding his knowledge of the written records from those days and of the terrain itself, something of the nature of the people who lived there.

We can all find in these amazingly crisp images an immediately comprehensible record of the major accom-plishments of the Haidas who, through their genius, in-genuity, dedication, and energy, transcended their lack of numbers and sophisticated technical resources and or-ganization to make an outstanding contribution to the sum of human achievement.

Of course, when these pictures were made, the great days of the Haidas were already over. The occasional hu-man to be seen was one of a tragically small remnant to survive the destruction of their people. What we see are the ghosts of villages, homes of ghost people. Even the great heraldic beasts, monsters, and humans of the totem poles are now ghosts. But what lively, powerful ghosts those old demigods still are, and the raven at least seems alive, well, and waiting.

Bill Reid

Facing page: The Raven and the First Men **by modern Haida carver Bill Reid, illustrating the story of how Raven brought mankind to consciousness by freeing them from a clamshell.** *McLennan* (UBCMA)

PREFACE

SINCE THE APPEARANCE OF *Haida Monumental Art* in 1983, from which this work was drawn, there has been much loss of both sites and monuments by the hand of man and the forces of nature on the Queen Charlotte Islands. Important carved poles have fallen to the ground at the abandoned villages of Skedans and Tanu, and even in the inhabited village of Skidegate, the last of the old poles was brought down by a windstorm and smashed. Many other old sites have been denuded of their forest setting by logging operations that have swept much of the islands since research for this book began in 1966.

In contrast to this loss there have been some very positive gains as well since the 1983 publication. The village of Ninstints, the gem of the old villages, has been carefully cleared of undergrowth and the poles stabilized with the most advanced conservation techniques by the staffs of the Royal British Columbia Museum in Victoria and the Canadian Conservation Institute and Parks Canada, Ottawa. Ninstints has also been declared a site of importance to the heritage of mankind by the World Heritage Site Committee of UNESCO.

Of particular importance has been the recent decision of the Minister of the Environment of the Government of Canada to establish a park to protect both the natural and cultural heritage of the Southern Queen Charlotte Islands from further logging operations. The major villages of Ninstints, Tanu, and Skedans are included in this area as well as the smaller village site of Kaidju. The Chairman of the National Historic Board, Professor Tom Symons, deserves particular credit in my view for achieving this level of protection, as does Miles Richardson of Skidegate and many other Haida elders and youth who fought to save the heritage of their ancestors. It will be a major challenge for both heritage agencies and the Haida

people to develop an approach that will allow visitors to the Queen Charlotte Islands to see and enjoy the magnificent sites and remain without destroying them for future generations. With proper planning, I believe the old villages can attract culturally sensitive tourists whose economic input will offset most of the income lost to logging. The sustained yield of the heritage sites will benefit the regional economy in the long term. The renewal of Haida artistic traditions can do the rest.

Those great traditions in sculpting in wood, bone, and precious metals are also rapidly developing in directions hardly expected five years ago. Bill Reid's monumental sculptures of a killer whale as well as his Spirit Messenger sculpture will grace the portals of the Grand Hall at the new Canadian Museum of Civilization in Ottawa, through the generous donations of Mr. and Mrs. James Graham and of Tele-Globe Canada, respectively. His fabulous bronze Spirit Canoe will soon be headed down Pennsylvania Avenue towards the White House at the new Canadian embassy in Washington. A younger generation of artists led by Robert Davidson is also making the world aware of the serene beauty of Haida art. The future of Haida culture looks immensely brighter towards the close of the century than it did at the beginning.

I would like to thank Dr. Margaret Hess of Calgary for much encouragement and support in the publishing of this volume. I would also thank Dr. Michael Ames, Director of the Museum of Anthropology at UBC, and the staff of UBC Press, particularly Brian Scrivener, for steering this work to its conclusion and finally my wife, Joanne, and children Christine and Grant for their support and sacrifices en route.

George F. MacDonald

Facing page: **Photographer Hannah Maynard, who taught her husband Richard the skills he used to record the art and architecture of the Northwest Coast tribes, photographed at Haina.** *Maynard* **1888** (CMC 100461)

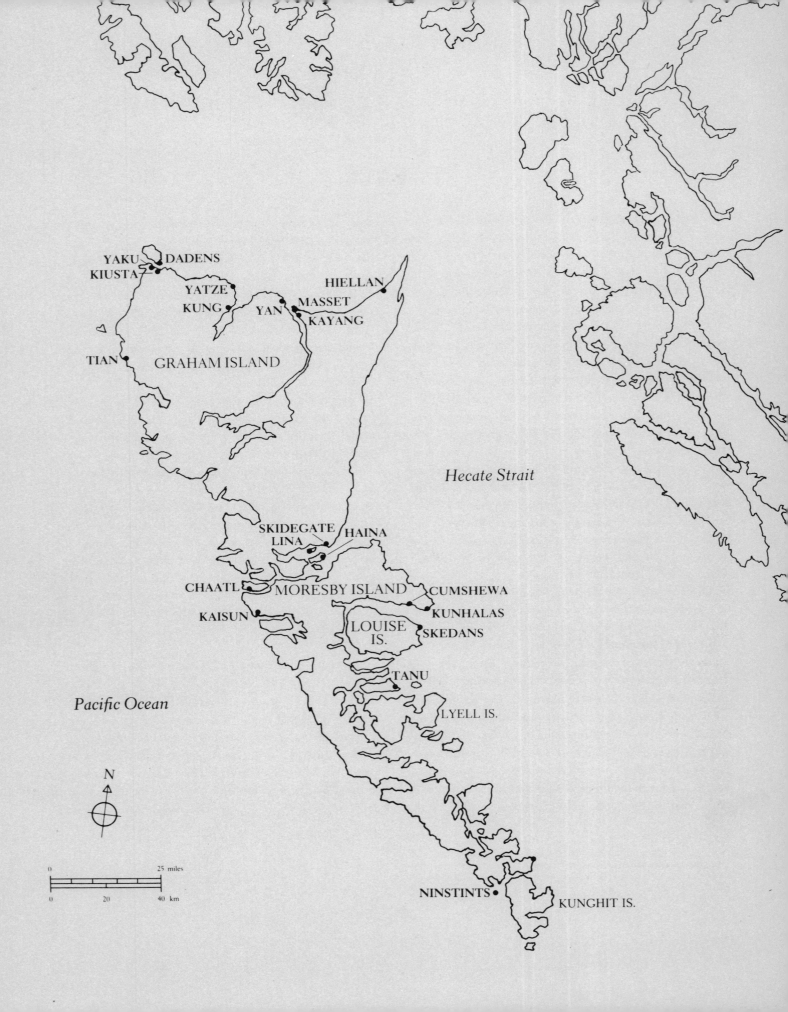

YAKU — DADENS
KIUSTA

YATZE
KUNG   YAN   HIELLAN
                MASSET
                KAYANG

TIAN   GRAHAM ISLAND

Hecate Strait

SKIDEGATE   HAINA
LINA

CHAATL   MORESBY ISLAND   CUMSHEWA
                        KUNHALAS
KAISUN   LOUISE   SKEDANS
            IS.

            TANU

Pacific Ocean   LYELL IS.

N

0   25 miles
0   20   40 km

NINSTINTS   KUNGHIT IS.

INTRODUCTION

ARCHAEOLOGY · TRADITIONAL SOCIETY
COSMOLOGY · MYTHOLOGY · CONTACT
WITH EUROPEAN CULTURE · HAIDA
DWELLINGS · CRESTS · THE HOUSE
FRONTAL POLE · MORTUARY SCULPTURE
MEMORIAL POLES · ETHNOGRAPHY
AMONG THE HAIDA · PICTURE SOURCES

Facing page: **The Queen Charlotte Islands showing
Haida heritage site locations**

Skidegate, showing the proudly decorated fringe between forest and seashore on which the Haida dwelt. *Dawson, 1878* (CMC 255)

INTRODUCTION

TO THE HAIDA their world was like the edge of a knife cutting between the depths of the sea, which to them symbolized the underworld, and the forested mountainsides, which marked the transition to the upper world. For the most part the Haida lived in isolated villages of a few hundred people, in communal dwellings strung in a thin line along narrow stretches of beach or rock-bound coves. On the one side they faced treacherous ocean currents; on the other, dense forests.

Perhaps because of their precarious position, they embellished the narrow human zone of their villages with a profusion of boldly carved monuments and brightly painted emblems signifying their identity. Throughout their villages these representations of the creatures of the upper and lower worlds presented a balanced statement of the forces of their universe. Animals and birds represented the upper world of the forest and the heavens, while sea mammals, especially killer whales, and fishes symbolized the underworld. The transition between realms was bridged by such amphibians as frogs, beavers, and otters. Hybrid mythological creatures, such as sea grizzlies and sea wolves, symbolized a merging of cosmic zones.

ARCHAEOLOGY

The earliest archaeological evidence of human habitation on the Queen Charlotte Islands has been dated to about 7,000 years ago, although evidence from elsewhere on the north Pacific coast suggests that first settlement could have begun closer to 10,000 years ago. At first, people probably lived in small family bands in temporary structures built of poles and hides. The first inhabitants likely hunted land mammals, particularly caribou, of which a distinct subspecies survived on the Islands until the twentieth century. Sea mammals, salmon, and other fish that abound in the waters around the Islands were also taken as food.

Accumulations of shell refuse and animal bones, some dating from about 5,000 years ago, stretch along ancient beaches which lie behind the modern shore. This suggests that a village pattern of a single row of communal dwellings facing the water developed early. One site, at Blue Jacket Creek on the east coast of Masset Inlet, has yielded evidence, dating back over 3,500 years, of well-developed woodworking tools, such as wedges and hammers for splitting planks from the straight-grained red cedar of the Islands, and adze and chisel blades for finishing the planks. Also found were bone fishhook barbs, barbed harpoon heads, and ground slate lance heads used in the hunt.

Through the centuries new tools and techniques for woodworking, hunting, and fishing were added, either by local innovation or borrowing from neighbouring tribes. Slowly this culture was transformed into what we know as the Haida.

TRADITIONAL SOCIETY

The Haida divided themselves into two groups (what anthropologists term "moieties") called the Ravens and the Eagles, primarily for the regulation of marriages; all marriage partners had to be chosen from the opposite moiety. Each moiety was in turn subdivided into numerous localized sub-groups or lineages. Each lineage customarily took its name from the village it originally inhabited. Finally, a lineage would be further subdivided into as many as a dozen separate households, whose members occupied a common dwelling and recognized the authority of a house chief. A lineage chief was

Facing page: "Lively, powerful ghosts... the great totem poles of the Haidas." Abandoned poles at Yan. *Dorsey* 1897 (CMC J-20964-4)

simply the head of the leading household of that lineage by virtue of his wealth or prestige.

Descent was reckoned through the female line, so that the house chief might be an Eagle, while his wife and their children would be Ravens. A chief's property and privileges were inherited by his sister's sons, while his own sons inherited the property of his wife's brother, although in the event that a deceased man was survived by his brothers, their claim took precedence.

Two classes of people were recognized in Haida society. The nobility, or upper class, were those whose parents had provided "potlatches"—feasts accompanied by the distribution of wealth—to enhance their prestige. Higher social rank was seldom acquired by an individual directly through his acts or acquisition of wealth. However, a more elevated rank would be conferred upon his successors. Slaves, usually captives from rival villages or native groups, were considered to be outside the social order.

Wealth consisted of the right of access to both natural and supernatural resources. Rights and privileges belonged to the lineage and were exercised by the lineage chief. They might include rights to hunting lands or fishing streams, rocky islets where sea mammals could be clubbed, berry-picking areas, stands of fine timber, or stretches of beach where whales might be stranded. Each lineage had a founding ancestor and a history which was the basis for claiming these rights and privileges. Linking the lineage with the ancestral and supernatural sources of power were the songs, dances, crests for use in carving, and names belonging to the lineage.

An individual acquired new names at different times throughout life and had alternate names at any one time. Names defined a person's position within a community and validated his status. They provided a link to his lineage and his ancestors, and they were a statement of contact with the supernatural. Besides his personal name, a chief possessed a name which served as a title of his office. This name would be conferred upon the new chief at the potlatch marking his predecessor's death. In some cases different names were used for alternate generations of chiefs, but their use still designated the continuity of that line of house, family, or village chiefs.

COSMOLOGY

The Haida cosmos is divided into three zones: the sky world, the earth, and the underworld. The Haida conceive of the earth as a flat, circular form over which hangs a solid firmament, very like a bowl inverted over a plate. The earth consists of two islands: Haida Land (the Queen Charlotte Islands) and Seaward Country (the mainland).

Haida Land is supported by a supernatural being called Sacred-One-Standing-and-Moving, who rests on a copper box. On his breast is a pole or pillar that supports Haida Land and extends through a hole in the top of the firmament into the sky world above. The pole he supports can be visualized as a great cedar tree that grows at the centre of Haida Land. To the Haida, the cosmic tree is a living being that unites the three main zones of the cosmos: its roots penetrate into the underworld; its trunk extends from the earth; and its branches spread into the firmament. Power flows through the world pole. On the domestic scale the world pole or tree is represented by the carved house pole, which is a ceremonial conduit of power.

The Haida believe the land to be mostly underlain by water, and it is thought that killer whales or supernatural water beings can surface in lakes far inland from the sea.

At times the vault of heaven is thought to be an enormous skin tent. At other times it is said to be like an enormous plank house, into which the sun enters through the front door each morning and leaves by the back door at night. The stars are the light of the sun coming through holes in the roof of the celestial house, as the sun circles back overhead to its starting point at the front of the house. The Haida kept calendars by marking the place on the house wall where sunlight from a crack in the opposite wall fell each day of the year.

Above the sky door there are five additional layers of the cosmos, each with its own society and its own celestial house at the centre. The same series of five levels is repeated in the underworld. The crucial thing is to maintain harmony between these cosmic zones, for disharmony in any one is reflected in an unfortunate event in the human world, such as the failure of a fish run or other natural disasters.

The Haida classified and ranked all creatures, both natural and supernatural. In the mineral kingdom, metals stood at the top of the hierarchy. Copper had the highest rank. It was the noble metal of the Haida, and a shield made of copper was their most important object of symbolic wealth. Most important in the vegetable kingdom was the red cedar tree, which provided houses, clothing, utensils, and canoes.

The animal kingdom was of paramount importance to the Haida and consequently was the most carefully observed and classified. Animals were divided into sea creatures, land creatures, and sky creatures. The killer whales were the chiefs of the seals and other sea creatures, the bear was chief of land mammals, and the eagle the chief of sky beings. Each chief controlled the numbers and movements of the species under his control. Human beings had to compensate ritually the masters of the other creatures with prayers and offerings of food in order to ensure successful hunting, fishing, or food gathering.

Because animals were thought to possess souls of the same type as humans, they were classified as people with special attributes and abilities. There were bear people, raven people, and killer whale people, just as there were Haida people. Each category was organized into two social groups or moieties on the same basis as the Haida themselves. Some animals were assigned to the Eagle moiety, others to the Raven. Animals had their own territories, villages, houses, canoes, and chiefs. In their own houses, they used human form, and when they wished to appear in their animal form they put on cloaks and masks and spoke their animal language. Myths frequently tell of heroes being escorted by spirit beings to a village of people who at some stage betray the fact that they are really bear people or salmon people. When Haida put on animal masks and cloaks during rituals and carefully mimicked the grunts, howls, and calls of animals or birds, they entered a mental state in which they believed they had become part of the animal society.

Occasionally humans had supernatural experiences in the woods or out at sea which took them to the houses of the chief and chieftainess of the salmon, or other supernatural creatures. Such a visit to the house of a supernatural being brought wealth in various forms to the traveller.

The Haida believed in reincarnation. The souls of the dead made their abode between incarnations on earth in the houses of the supernatural chiefs. Haida children, particularly those of noble birth, were always closely scrutinized at birth to see whom they were reincarnating. Since all ancestors are stationed at times in the houses of the supernatural chiefs who control all the world's wealth, they have influence with these chiefs. If they are pleased with the honour their names receive in the potlatches and with the frequency of small gifts of

Two Skidegate chiefs attired in European style. *Dossetter, 1881* (AMNH 42263)

An old woman of Haina with a lower lip plug, symbol of high rank.
Dossetter, 1881 (AMNH 42270)

food that are sent to them through the smoke of the central hearth, the ancestors will procure better fish runs and other favours from the supernatural chief for their earthbound kin.

MYTHOLOGY

The mythology of the Haida, like their sculpture and painting, is based on the grand themes found throughout the Northwest Coast area, but the Haida added their own embellishments to each of these expressive traditions. Haida myths can be arranged into various sets, the most important of which is the Raven cycle.

In the beginning of the Raven cycle of myths, chaos is portrayed by the existence of a single reef near what would later be the town of Ninstints. On this reef, which lies between the boundless expanse of the sea and the sky, all of the supernatural beings are heaped up like piles of driftwood. Raven creates the Queen Charlotte Islands out of a black pebble and the mainland out of a white, crystalline one. The supernatural beings immediately leave their crowded reef and swim over to the Islands.

Throughout this first cycle Raven obtains elements of the universe from other beings. He is rarely a prime creator but more often a transposer and transformer who is responsible more for the present order of the universe than for the origin of its components. The Haida themselves Raven releases from a clamshell which he has dug out of the ground at Rose Spit.

A central theme of the second cycle of Raven myths is the acquisition and control of food resources. In his travels Raven is often accompanied by Eagle, which establishes a basis for the moiety divisions of Eagle and Raven; the two are often in direct competition for food.

Although the Raven cycle is dominant among Haida myths, there is another category of myth, individual myths based on archetypal themes. Many of these classic myths involve marriage alliances and access to wealth. Several recur in the crest carvings on poles, where they affirm the rights and privileges of the pole owner and his family.

CONTACT WITH EUROPEAN CULTURE

The Haida interpreted the first European ships to visit them as floating houses containing great wealth, sent by the ancestors, and manned by ghosts. The appearance of the Europeans and their sailing ships matched Haida traditions of encounters with supernatural beings almost exactly. Many legends told of fishermen out in their canoes who had come face-to-face with beings who controlled all the wealth of the sea. this view was reinforced once the true wealth of these strange new beings, in iron, copper, and other highly coveted objects, was revealed. The puzzled Europeans were met by the Haida and other Northwest Coast tribes with ritual greeting gestures and songs of welcome intended for meetings with the supernatural.

The first European visitors to the Queen Charlotte Islands were the Spanish, beginning with Juan Pérez, who traded with the Haida from his ship, *Santiago,* near Langara Island in 1774. Early Spanish and Russian expeditions to the area uncovered the rich fur trade potential of the north Pacific coast, particularly for the fine pelts of the sea otter. It was George Dixon, trading for the King George's Sound Company, who, in 1787, named the islands after Charlotte, queen to King George III of England. Anchored just south of Cape Santa Margarita, Dixon's purser William Beresford recorded: "In less than half an hour, we had purchased three hundred of the finest pelts we had ever seen." By the time Dixon had circumnavigated the island group he had traded for some 2,000 skins, which brought a high price in the markets of Macao. When news of this bonanza got out, the Queen Charlotte Islands became the hub of fur trading activity on the north Pacific coast, and for the next four decades they were visited by hundreds of European and American ships.

The Haida had honed their trading skills during centuries of formal trade with surrounding tribes to acquire items foreign to the Queen Charlottes, such as copper, mountain goat wool, and the rich oil of the oolichan fish. Traders' journals abound with accounts of the shrewd trading tactics of the Haida chiefs. Captains had to set their crews to sewing clothing from sailcloth, their carpenters to making furniture, and their blacksmiths to forging adzes or hardware to meet the requests of demanding Haida traders. Some ships were even forced to trade their stores to other natives farther south on the coast for elk hides or ornamental shells to meet the Haida's requirements.

The introduction of European metal woodworking tools had a major influence on Haida material culture. Metal tools allowed the expression of Haida monumental art and architecture on a scale previously not possible, although it appears that the styles and prototypes had been worked out through many centuries of village life on the Queen Charlottes and elsewhere on the Northwest Coast.

At the beginning of the 1830s the decline of the sea otter trade created a sudden scarcity of European goods. Haida could no longer rely on the visits of traders' ships but were forced to travel to the new Hudson's Bay Company post on the mainland at Fort Simpson.

The opening of Fort Simpson also altered the pattern of warfare on the coast. The Coast Tsimshian, long the target of Haida raids, were secure under the guns of the fort. The interests of the Hudson's Bay Company, as well as those of the Russian American Company at Sitka to the north, were in commerce, not warfare. Both companies tried to discourage warfare. As warfare waned, potlatching—"fighting with property"—developed as a substitute. Hard on the heels of the Hudson's Bay Company traders came settlers and missionaries.

In the late 1830s the first of a series of smallpox epidemics ravaged the Northwest Coast, affecting virtually every Haida village. About half the Haida had died by the end of the decade.

During the 1840s trade among the Haida was monopolized by fewer and fewer chiefs. Among the southern Haida the major chiefs were forced by the failing circumstances of their remote location and dwindling population to accept the paramountcy of Chief Skidegate by about 1850. In the north, even the powerful Chief Edenshaw of Kiusta came under the domination of Chief Wiah at Masset. Rapid population decline through disease, especially the apocalyptic epidemic of 1862–3, and growing reliance on trade led the Haida to abandon the more remote villages, until only Skidegate and Masset remained by the end of the nineteenth century.

HAIDA DWELLINGS *The House as Symbol*

The Haida plank house could function in the secular realm as a dwelling as well as in the spiritual realm as a ceremonial centre. It was the abode of the living as well as an embodiment of their ancestors. On ceremonial occasions one entered into the body of the ancestor through its mouth, the oval entryway cut through the crest animal at the base of the frontal pole. Houses symbolized the house lineage, and entering into them marked a clear transition from the profane world to the spiritual world of the ancestors, bringing the Haida into intimate association with their cultural traditions.

At the same time, the house was a manifestation of the cosmos. The house contained human social life in the same way that the universe contained the natural world.

The house structure could be comprehended by the individual, while the cosmos could not, so it helped people's understanding to impose the structure of the house, with its floor, supports, and protective roof, on the universe, with its pillars and vault of heaven.

The alignment of houses in the village was based upon social rank, ideally with the houses of the more prestigious chiefs arrayed on either side of the house of the village chief, which occupied a central location in the house row. Although most villages show this distribution, migration of lineages from village to village disrupted the ideal alignment.

Almost all villages contained households belonging to lineages from both moieties, which were grouped together according to the historic development of the village. Each house was established on what, for the lineage that owned it, was the symbolic centre of the world. A line representing the middle world dominated by mankind was connected from house to house, the whole length of the village. This line marked the intersection of the underworld—the sea which the houses faced across a thin strand of beach—and the upper world, accessible through the forested hillsides behind the village. A separate axis ran from the sea world to the sky world through the centre of each house. The two lines met at the house pit, the absolute centre of each lineage's world, which was the ritual focus for ceremonies held in the house.

House Types

The Haida built two types of houses, which differed mainly in the approach to construction, rather than in the character of the finished house. *Type 1* is a simple support structure of two parallel round beams set on pairs of uprights. To this basic structure is added a framework of light rafters, sills, corner posts, and gables, which is then covered with planks. There is little

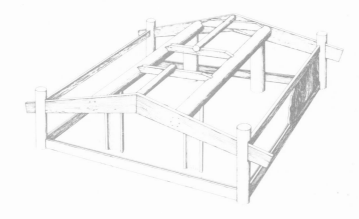

Type 1 house frame

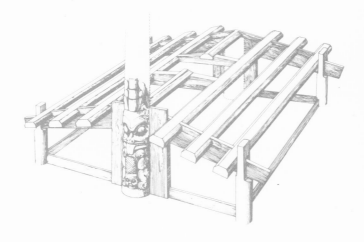

Type 2 house frame

The post-and-beam construction shows clearly in this house, as does the intricate decoration of the carved interior post and painted chief's bench. (RBCM E118)

integration between massive frame and light covering.

House *type 2* integrates all the structural members and distributes the stress by employing more elaborate joinery, including mortise-and-tenon joints and interlocking features. The extensive use of joinery in the house, with supports integrated into the walls, adds strength to the structure and provides more interior space.

Among all other cultures on the Northwest Coast, all houses are of *type 1*. Among the Haida, distribution of *type 2* houses ranges from almost none in the Alaskan villages of the Kaigani Haida to an overwhelming majority in the southern villages, particularly Ninstints. This suggests that *type 1* was the original form of house construction and that the *type 2* style was a specialized later development which originated in the southern villages. The Haida may have modelled the joinery of *type 2* houses after fittings seen on board European ships, since the construction details bear little relationship to the traditional principles of Haida joinery.

House Building

When a high-ranking chief had accumulated the wealth required to raise a house, he contracted with people of the opposite moiety to assemble the building materials. Work parties set out in groups of thirty or forty in five- or six-man canoes to the cutting site. All would paddle strongly, singing songs in time with the paddle strokes, led by the man in the bow.

The site selected for cutting timbers was either one which belonged to the family of the chief building the house or one for which he had paid another family for the privilege of cutting timbers. On an earlier reconnaissance of the area, the chief had selected the trees to be cut. Special care was taken in the selection of trees for the frontal poles and roof beams. Working in relays, the men cut the trees as quickly as possible. Planks were cut from the trees on the site.

Once the building materials had been prepared in the forest, the planks were loaded onto canoes, and the logs for the frontal poles, posts, and beams were towed back to the village. Upon arrival the planks were trimmed down further with steel adzes or, in prehistoric times, the sharpened shells of the large California blue mussel. Planks that were to be painted were smoothed with stone abraders and polished with the rough skin of the dogfish.

If the house was to have an interior pit another day's effort with digging sticks and baskets was necessary. The holes for the frontal pole and support posts were also dug that day.

Once the major structural beams for the house were erected, sheeting for the house frame was added, starting with the floor planking, running from the house pit to the walls. Next the wall boards were inserted into slots in the underside of the top plate and gables, and the bottoms of the boards were swung into gaps that were made in the sills. The boards were then slid into position. The last plank in each wall was secured by batten strips on the sills which could be removed to provide a temporary opening in a wall on certain occasions, such as the removal of the dead or the entry of feast performers. If an interior bench was intended, it was built of planks after the wall boards had been inserted.

In the roof, above the central hearth, was the smoke hole. Over the hole was placed a cover which prevented the heavy rainfall of the Islands from falling on the hearth area. Sacrifices, particularly bits of food or oil, were thrown into the fire to be carried aloft as smoke to the celestial houses of the supernatural ones.

In their journal, published in 1801, Captain Chanal and Surgeon Roblet provide a description of the interior of a finished house in Dadens:

The fire is placed in the middle of the edifice; there it is that food is dressed. This same apartment, fifty feet long, serves at once for kitchen, dining-room, bed chamber, stove house, and workshop, and also as a shed for the canoe, when she is not employed afloat. While on one side, some women are giving their attention to the children and to the family concerns, some, elsewhere, are drying and smoking fish for winter stock; and others are busied in making mats, and joining and sewing furs in order to make them into cloaks. No fixed places were distinguishable for sleeping, and according to appearances, all the individuals of a family sleep pell-mell on the boarded floor. . . . the youngest are laid in cradles suspended like hammocks. Our voyageurs saw a number of chests piled up on the sides and in the corners of the habitation, and they learnt that these chests hold their winter provisions, and that, in others, are contained bows and arrows. In different places on the walls, were hung darts, lances, nets, fish-hooks, with poles and lines for fishing. The habitations are, in general, painted and decorated in various ways. (Howay 1925:293)

House Decoration

Many parts of the house could be decorated or carved. Such elaboration was strictly controlled by the status of the house chief. Each embellishment was considered a prerogative of rank, so that the house chief had to be able to afford both their execution by artists and their validation by his fellow villagers through ceremonies.

CRESTS

Although at first glance all the crests on Haida poles and monuments appear to depict animals, some represent natural phenomena, such as the clouds or the rainbow, as well as supernatural beings, such as the mythic floating tree snag Tcama'os. Most crests are, however, rendered in an animal form.

Ideally, each moiety should have had crests that were unique and which would have separated it clearly from the other. To some extent this was true, but some transfer of crests occurred between moieties on both the north and south islands. Not all families were entitled to use all the crests controlled by their moiety; crests were jealously guarded. Through the potlatch new crests could be introduced in the form of a mask, a tattoo design, or a house post motif.

Raven crests included, among many others, the killer whale, grizzly bear, thunderbird, black bear, mountain goat, and moon. Eagle crests included the eagle, frog, beaver, and raven.

THE HOUSE FRONTAL POLE

The most obvious ornamented house member was the frontal pole or *gayang*. The artist commissioned to design and carve a frontal pole usually belonged to the opposite moiety from the chief building the house. The craft was hereditary; a boy would learn his skill by long apprenticeship with his maternal uncle. A master carver closely supervised the work of his apprentices. Often he did one side of the pole himself and left the other side for the apprentice to copy, but always under the master's watchful eye.

The features of the figures on the poles were always painted in black, red, and blue, and occasionally, in the late period, white. But within ten to twelve years, to judge from photographs of the same poles at different times, all but faint traces of paint disappeared. On rare occasions square plaques of abalone shell were inset and glued on the poles.

The raising of a frontal pole was accompanied by a special potlatch. The pole raising was done by members of the opposite moiety from the owner of the house.

They were paid liberally for their efforts by the distribution of goods at the feast, as were the carver and his assistants.

Rarely, house fronts were painted or carved, or both. Other houses had painted screens that could be attached to the front of the house for ceremonial occasions.

Front corner posts were occasionally carved, usually with small watchman figures, or less frequently with eagles or ravens. The front ends of purlins were carved in rare instances as sea lions, bears, or human figures. Interior posts at the rear of the house were frequently carved or painted. For ceremonial occasions carved and painted screens were often added to create a secluded room at the back of the house.

MORTUARY SCULPTURE

Family mortuary houses, located behind the family's dwelling, were predominantly shed-roofed. They bore a frontal plaque emblazoned with a painting symbolic of the creatures of the upper and lower worlds or of some transitional form, such as the sea grizzly or sea wolf. Carved birds, usually thunderbirds, can be seen in photographs atop many of the mortuary houses. A second, rare type of mortuary was a gable-roofed structure, essentially a miniature version of a *type 2* dwelling, with a small frontal pole and overhanging roof beams.

Freestanding sculpted crest figures, or *mandas*, depicted supernatural killer whales, sculpins, or sea grizzlies, which are transitional figures found both on land and in the water. Undoubtedly their task was to bear the dead to the underworld.

The mortuary pole, which the Haida called a *xat*, meaning "grandfather," was usually a stout post, hollowed out at the top to receive the grave box of a chief. A front plaque, decorated with a crest, sealed the front of the chamber, and a similar plank formed the roof.

Right: **Beaver manda from Eagle House, Skedans**
(AMNH 318934)

Below: **The frontal pole of this mortuary house
from Cumshewa bears a halibut crest.** (CFM
16246)

Left: **This interior post from Skidegate illustrates the thunderbird crest.** *Dossetter,* 1881 (AMNH 42288)

Below: **Stereo photo of Masset taken by Richard Maynard, 1884** (RBCM VII.B.33)

Left: **Haida shaman in ceremonial regalia, holding the rattle used in conjuring** (RBCM)

PHOTOGRAPHED BY R. MAYNARD.

VICTORIA, B. C.

MEMORIAL POLES

To honour relatives whose remains were deposited elsewhere, particularly those who had drowned and whose bodies were never recovered, tall poles were set up as memorials. They generally had a single crest figure at the base and often a separate figure of an eagle or raven on the top.

ETHNOGRAPHY AMONG THE HAIDA

The ethnographic record of the Haida is limited in comparison with that of other important Northwest Coast tribes. Many observations exist only as fragmentary field notes, hastily written down during a few hours or days spent at village sites. In most cases, information concerning house ownership and family affiliation was related by survivors who had gathered at the two great villages of Skidegate and Masset many years after the villages concerned had been abandoned and their people decimated or dispersed. Some informants had personal knowledge of the individuals and events, but more often they recounted what they had heard from relatives and acquaintances. Thus, the record of the Haida villages is incomplete and full details of family and individual history are lost beyond recovery. In addition, the distortions of recollection and the selective bias of personal enmity or interfamily rivalry may have played a part in the interpretation of events which the informants made for the ethnographers.

The identifications of houses and their owners made in this book are based on these imperfect data, mostly on the field notes of John Swanton, a professional ethnographer for the Bureau of American Ethnology, Smithsonian Institution, who compiled village house lists from survivors in Masset from 1900 to 1901, and Charles Newcombe, a medical doctor and collector of native artifacts who between 1897 and 1913 visited virtually all the abandoned villages of the Haida and made sketch maps, photographs, and drawings keyed to detailed written descriptions and identifications. Village descriptions also rely on the observations of other travellers, including George Mercer Dawson, a geologist employed by the Geological Survey of Canada who spent the summer of 1878 surveying the entire periphery of the Islands, making both geological and ethnographic observations. The estimates of village population are largely based on a census carried out between 1836 and 1841 by John Work, a Hudson's Bay employee based at Fort Simpson. An attempt has been made to reconcile conflicting information where confirmation from another source was available, but this has not always been possible, and doubtless some contradictions still exist.

Tattooed Haida from Skidegate. On his chest is a tattoo of a brown bear; on each wrist, a dogfish. *Niblack* 1886 (SI 4117)

THE SOUTHERN

HAINA · CUMSH

NINSTIN

VILLAGES: SKIDEGATE
EWA · SKEDANS · TANU
S · KAISUN · CHAATL

SKIDEGATE LIES ON A LONG STRETCH OF BEACH on the north shore of the entrance of Skidegate Inlet. Freshwater streams define the eastern and western boundaries of the village, and behind it is a terrace which marks an ancient beach line from the end of the last Ice Age. Beyond that are heavily wooded hills and the small lakes which, in Haida mythology are said to be inhabited by water monsters.

The village was named by the early traders after the town chief, Skidegate, or "Son of the chiton," although the name by which the Haida called their village probably translates as "Place of stones." The town was originally owned by a Raven lineage, who gave the town to an Eagle lineage as payment for an injury done to one of the latter's members.

The first recorded contact between Europeans and the people of Skidegate was made by Captain George Dixon, who anchored in July 1787 off the entrance to Skidegate Inlet. Although Dixon did not visit the village he provides the first description of Chief Skidegate:

> *Of all the Indians we have seen, this chief had the most savage aspect, and his whole appearance sufficiently marked him as a proper person to lead a tribe of cannibals. His stature was above the common size; his body spare and thin, and though at first sight he appeared lank and emaciated, yet his step was bold and firm, and his limbs apparently strong and muscular; his eyes were large and goggling, and seemed ready to start out of their sockets; his forehead deeply wrinkled, not merely by age, but from a continual frown; all this, joined to a long visage, hollow cheeks, high, elevated cheek bones, and a natural ferocity of temper, formed a countenance not easily beheld without some degree of emotion. However, he proved very useful in conducting our traffic with his people, and the intelligence he gave us, and the methods he took to make himself understood, showed him to possess a strong natural capacity. (1789:115–17)*

Above: **House corner posts ridiculing Judge Pemberton of the Victoria Police Court (left) and George Smith, Victoria town clerk. They were carved to erase the indignity caused by the imprisonment of the chief of this house early in the 1870s.** (CFM 93087)

Facing page: **Houses 20 to 22 (from right). A raven, with beak protruding, can be seen at the base of the middle house frontal pole (House 21).** *Dawson 1878* (NAC 255)

Left: **Map showing house and pole positions.**
*Maps are not to scale

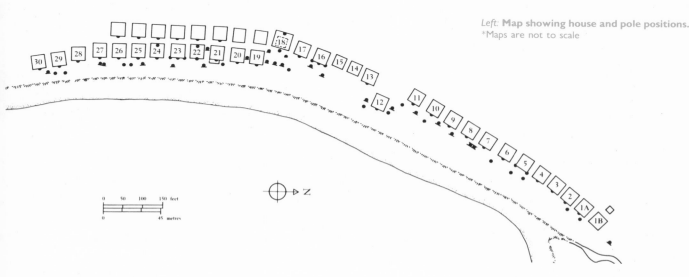

After the flurry of the sea otter trade had passed, few ships visited Skidegate until the arrival of the whalers who wintered near the village for a few years in the 1830s. At least one whaling captain, a Mr. Jefferson, made his permanent residence in the village and married a daughter of the chief. In 1834 a Hudson's Bay Company post was established at Fort Simpson on the mainland, and from the outset the chiefs at Skidegate monopolized the trade from the villages further west on Skidegate Inlet, whose traders had to pass by their village.

The discovery of gold in the Queen Charlotte Islands in 1850 brought the first mass influx of whites. However, first indications of a large deposit were not fulfilled, and by 1854 the gold rush had subsided. A number of ships visited the area in search of gold, and two of them were wrecked. Their crews were made prisoner and later taken to Fort Simpson, where they were ransomed by the Hudson's Bay Company. The Skidegate chiefs made considerable money in the brief gold rush and from the ransom of the sailors. This windfall led to a flurry of raising new poles and building new houses. It also culminated in a bad reputation for the people of Skidegate, with the result that no ships visited them for some time.

The lack of trading contacts bothered the Haida, and in 1853 five hundred villagers left the Islands to see for themselves the growing settlements of Victoria and Nanaimo. Their arrival in Victoria frightened its residents, and the Haida were sent home by Governor James Douglas, but not before they had assessed the opportunities for trade and work. A few weeks later five canoes, carrying mostly men, arrived quietly back in Victoria. This started an annual migration that lasted for two decades and left Skidegate almost abandoned for much of the year. The returning families brought back two things, both of which affected the village drastically. One was the wealth they had accumulated, which allowed them to build larger and more elaborate houses and monuments. The other was a variety of diseases that raged through the village during the 1860s. It was only the arrival of people from other villages hit even harder by disease that kept Skidegate alive.

Missionaries came later to Skidegate than to other Northwest Coast villages. The Reverend W. H. Collison, who had established a mission at Masset, made only occasional visits to preach at Skidegate. His first encounter with the villagers was a memorable occasion for him:

> *They crowded in to see me until there was not standing room. Those who could do so mounted on the roof and peered down through the smoke hole. In the meantime food was being prepared, and, as soon as a common curiosity had been gratified, a great fire was erected on the hearth, con-*

Panorama showing the central and southwest part of Skidegate. *Dossetter* 1881 (AMNH 42264)

Left: **Thunder and Lightning House (House 16), showing the house front and its poles. The two watchman corner posts bracket the house frontal pole and a plain mortuary pole with the carved figure of a bear on top.** *Maynard, 1884 (BCARS 7344)*

Below: **A rare painted house front adorned Captain Gold's Moon House (House 31). Fastened to the peak of the house is a moon disk depicting the face of a thunderbird.** *Maynard, 1884 (CFM 17344)*

sisting of logs of four feet in length, over which frequent libations of fish grease were poured, until the flames issued above the roof, causing the spectators who had assembled to descend in dangerous haste. (1915:176)

A request to the Reverend William Duncan, who had established a prosperous mission at Metlakatla on the mainland opposite Skidegate, for a permanent Church Missionary Society preacher led to the assignment of a Tsimshian lay preacher. This did not please the Haida, so they went to the Methodist mission at Fort Simpson, which sent a white teacher, George Robinson, in 1883.

The effects of a permanent mission at Skidegate were rapid and profound. Within a year of Robinson's arrival, traditional plank houses were abandoned or demolished, to be replaced with single family dwellings of frame construction. The settlement pattern of the village was also changed to streets on a grid pattern in which the church became the major focus of community life. There is no evidence at Skidegate of any forced destruction of totem poles instigated by the missionaries as happened at Masset. Instead, the missionaries concentrated on replacing the communal dwellings, leaving the poles to eventual destruction through neglect and decay.

The date chosen for the village map is 1881. When in that year photographer Edward Dossetter stopped at Skidegate, several new houses were under construction and new memorial poles were being raised. This marked the end of the erection of traditional monuments at the village. By the time photographer Richard Maynard made his trip to Skidegate in 1884, most of the old houses had been pulled down or were in ruins, and many poles had fallen. The few remaining master carvers and builders received no new commissions after 1883. The people of Skidegate had decided to adopt the ways of the white man.

Left: The only historic pole still standing in Skidegate, this memorial was erected in 1882. The main crest figure is a beaver. 1963 (NFB PNN62)

HAINA

HAINA (NEW GOLD HARBOUR) is situated on the eastern end of Maude Island, only a few miles from Skidegate. Its name in Haida means "Sunshine Town." The site of Haina was said to have been the location of a prehistoric town.

In 1850, the discovery of gold near Chaatl brought the west coast villages into brief but intensive contact with white miners and traders. From these outsiders the villagers caught diseases, such as smallpox and tuberculosis, that decimated their populations. This misfortune forced the survivors to abandon their settlements and move closer to Skidegate. Coincident with this move was a desire to be closer to the Hudson's Bay Company posts on the mainland, particularly Fort Simpson.

Families from Kaisun (Old Gold Harbour) and Chaatl began to resettle in Haina as early as 1850. Haina was predominantly a Raven town, with seven of the ten identified houses belonging to that moiety. Although the Eagles were numerically inferior at Haina, the town chief, Ganai, was an Eagle. Raven and Eagle houses are intermixed throughout the house row. From photographic evidence, the village seems to have expanded towards the north, which may help to explain why the chief's house (House 3) is not at the centre of the village.

A fort called Sunshine Town Fort stood at the end of Lina Island opposite the village. Near it was a smaller village, House of Trouble, or Drum Village. Only one house survived there by 1911, owned by Chief Quians, who had brought the frontal pole from his old town of Chaatl.

In the face of further population decline, Haina was fully occupied for only about thirty years. In the 1880s the townspeople began to resettle in Skidegate. Houses continued to be built at Haina until near the end of the nineteenth century, when the village was abandoned. After 1884, the year represented in the map of the village, several small, single-family houses were built in European style with gabled roofs and sawn siding. A church was subsequently added behind the house row.

Above: **On the plaque of this mortuary is an elaborate sculpin design inlaid with abalone. Below it on the post are carved a raven and a heron.** *Maynard, 1884* (RBCM)

Facing page: **Chief "Highest peak in a mountain range" displays his coppers, symbols of wealth, in front of House Where People Always Want To Go (House 5). Draped over his shoulders is a Chilkat blanket, likely traded from the Tlingit.** *Maynard, 1888* (CFM 2734)

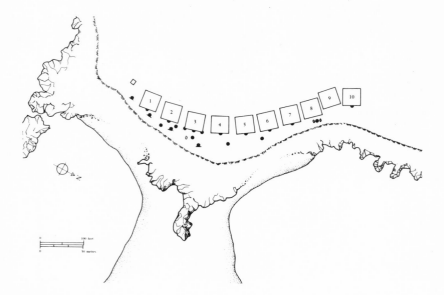

CUMSHEWA

CUMSHEWA WAS NAMED BY EUROPEANS after its chief, Gomshewah, whose name is probably a Bella Bella word meaning "Rich at the mouth of the river." In part, the term may refer to the wealth of salmon, herring, and oolichan which congregate at the mouths of rivers each year, and the seals, whales, and seabirds which follow the fish. A similar term is often used for high-ranking chiefs in reference to the supernatural beings who control the fish and animals, and whose houses are located near the river mouths. The Haida also initially used this term for Europeans because they associated their ships with these houses of wealth.

The village is located near the northern entrance to Cumshewa Inlet on a sandy beach. A long spit joins the village at low tide to Haans Islet, which was both a burial ground and the location of a fort. Behind the village the rocky land rises rapidly to over three hundred metres within two kilometres of the shore.

John Work estimated that there were twenty houses with 286 inhabitants at Cumshewa between 1836 and 1841, numbers which agree closely with the house list compiled by Swanton.

Cumshewa was inhabited almost exclusively by three closely related Eagle lineages. A single Raven lineage was present in one house, House 13. Several more houses were added in the late period after 1880, but they also appear to be Eagle houses.

Mortuary structures are more in evidence than at other villages. There are at least ten such buildings at Cumshewa, several of which had carved frontal poles of their own.

Just inside Cumshewa Head, opposite Cumshewa Island on the north entrance to Cumshewa Inlet, lay the small village of Kunhalas. Dawson found the ruins of a few houses when he visited the site in 1878.

When the Haida began to abandon many villages and resettle in Skidegate, Cumshewa was one of the last to be deserted. The map shows the village as it was about 1885. By 1905, Methodist missionaries were encouraging the last few inhabitants to move to Skidegate.

Facing page: **By the turn of the century, Cumshewa was only a fishing camp. Small sheds have been built among the remaining poles and skeletons of the former great frame houses. c1905** (UCA)

Above: **Mortuary box front from House 2. The central crest is a grizzly bear.** *Newcombe, 1897* (RBCM EC 30)

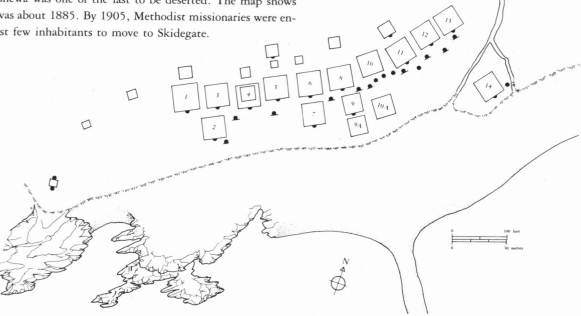

Poles associated with Sky House (House 11), which belonged to Chief Cumshewa. Note the coppers fastened to the memorial poles below the eagles' talons. *Dawson, 1878* (NAC 243)

To the right is Someone Lies Against It House (House 6) with its frontal pole. At left is the frontal pole to House 5, which was no longer standing. The mortuary post in the foreground was erected for the owner of House 6; on its crest plaque is a carved frog. *Dawson, 1878* (NAC 244)

SKEDANS

THE NAME SKEDANS IS A CORRUPTION by the early fur traders of the name of the head chief, Gida'nsta, which means "From his daughter," a title of respect used by children when addressing a person of high rank. The village had several other names as well, including Koona and Huadji-lanas ("Grizzly bear town"). Francis Poole, a civil and mining engineer with the Queen Charlotte Mining Company, wrote the following report of his visit with "Chief Klue" of Tanu to the "great chief of the Skiddan tribe" in 1863:

> *The high and mighty chief Skiddan sat in state. . . . He did not rise when I entered, but continued sitting on a rough kind of platform, with his legs crossed like a tailor's. I was invited to stand on his right, however. . . . The whole of the tribe then squatted down, also cross-legged, on some low benches or logs.*
>
> *Skidden himself delivered a grand speech, the general purport of which I gathered to be an advice and solemn injunction to his people to afford me every protection and assistance. They listened attentively, now and then interrupting Skiddan's harangue with queer uplifting of arms and murmurs of approbation, or with a sudden outburst of complimentary grunts directed at me.* (1872:108)

Facing page: **View of Skedans showing how the line of the house row follows the contour of the shoreline.** *Newcombe* **1902** (RBCM 227)

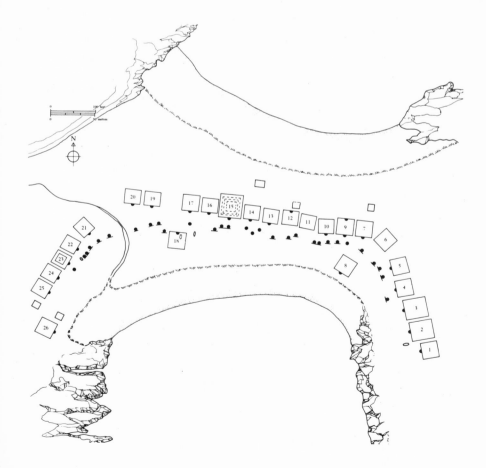

Through the friendship of an earlier Chief Skedans with Chief Tsebassa of Kitkatla, the people of Skedans had close ties with the Tsimshian people. A charter myth for the trading relationship between the two chiefs holds that they both had a common ancestor who migrated from the Nass. This trade introduced new customs, stories, and crests from the mainland.

John Work assigns to Skedans thirty houses and 738 inhabitants. In 1899 Swanton's informants recalled twenty-seven houses. There is physical evidence, on the ground and in photographs, of twenty-six houses, the number shown on the accompanying map.

The village faces south onto Skedans Bay from a small peninsula which ends in a high rocky prominence. In case of attack, villagers retreated to a fort built on this height of land. At the opposite end of the peninsula is a high rocky bluff filled with caves that were undoubtedly used as burial chambers.

Three Raven families dominated Skedans. All three shared the same crests. Two Eagle families also lived in the village. Almost all the crests of both clans figure in the village sculpture, as do other motifs depicting stories associated with the families.

Skedans was abandoned only a few years after Dawson's visit in 1878, at which time most of the houses appear to have been habitable.

Above: **In front of a grouping of mortuary poles sits a grizzly bear figure, which probably once bore the coffin of Xaosti, owner of House 2.** *Dawson, 1878* (NAC 248)

Below: **By 1947, the frontal pole for House Mother (House 24) had fallen. The top of the oval entryway can be seen in the belly of the grizzly bear crest at rear, the base of the frontal pole for Moon House (House 23).** *Barbeau, 1947* (CMC 102718)

Above: **The only poles that remained standing by 1901. Traces of paint can still be seen on the poles in the centre.** *Newcombe,* **1901** (RBCM E51)

TANU

TANU IS SITUATED ON A SIZEABLE ISLAND opposite Kunga Island in Las-keek Bay. The name T'anu refers to a type of sea grass found near the village. Another name was "Klue's village," after Xe-u, "Southeast," the original town chief and head of the ruling family. The village arrangement is unusual, in that it faces two beaches, and the house row is sharply divided by a rocky shoal.

John Work assigned forty houses and 545 inhabitants to this town in about 1840, while Swanton's informants in 1898 recalled only twenty-six houses. The National Museums of Canada Survey in 1968 uncovered evidence of twenty-five house sites. Judge Swan, who visited Tanu in 1883, counted thirty-one mortuary columns and fifteen mortuary houses in the village.

The first settlers at Tanu belonged to two closely aligned Eagle lineages who came from Cumshewa Inlet by way of Chicken Hawk Town, an ancestral village on Lyell Island. According to Swanton's informants, eleven chiefs had ruled at Tanu by the time the village was abandoned, which would suggest that, based on the average reign of ten to fifteen years recorded for the Skidegate chiefs, the village had been in existence for between 110 and 165 years prior to 1900, when the last chief, Gitkun, was known to have been living. Thus, Tanu probably does not date from earlier than 1735, in the period when movement of people on the Islands appears to have peaked in response to the first shock waves of European contact reaching the periphery of the Northwest Coast.

Strangely, the town chief belonged to an Eagle lineage with only one house in the village. Swanton theorized that this lineage was "one of the three or four greatest Eagle families on the Islands," and thus took aristocratic precedence over the other lineages in the village.

The town was abandoned after 1885, its people moving for a short period to New Klue (Church Creek), near the old story town of Djigua, before settling permanently in Skidegate.

Above: **This memorial was dedicated to the brother of the owner of Sea Lion House (House 6), who had drowned while hunting fur seal. It depicts a thunderbird clutching a whale.** *Newcombe,* **1902** (RBCM E232)

Facing page: **House-hole House (House 5).** *Newcombe,* **1902** (RBCM E285)

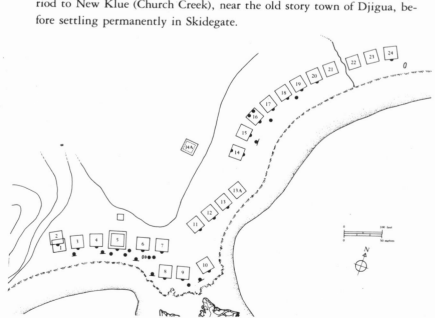

Preparations under way in July 1878 for a potlatch marking the erection of a new house and pole for the chief of Tanu. On the beach, behind the canoes, the carver can be seen putting the finishing touches on the new frontal pole. Behind him, a group of Tsimshian, who have just unloaded storage boxes at the door of the chief's new house, await the commencement of the feast. *Dawson, 1878* (NAC 242)

Interior pole of Easy To Enter House (House 14). The fierce crests portray (top) a sea grizzly with a seal poking between its ears and (base) a grizzly bear. *Newcombe, 1901* (RBCM E49)

Left: **This ancient, moss-encrusted pole lay at Kaidju in 1901.** *Newcombe, 1901* (RBCM E77)

Below: **Roof beams of Eagle House (House 17), flanking the eagle crest at the top of the frontal pole, were carved to resemble sea lion heads.** *Newcombe* (RBCM)

Ninstints

THE HAIDA NAME FOR THIS VILLAGE was Red Cod Island Town. The early European traders, however, named it after the head chief of the village, Nan stins ("He who is two"). It was probably this town that John Work referred to in his census by the name of Quee-ah, after an earlier chief, Koyah ("Raven"). Work assigned the village twenty houses and a population of 308 people. One of the last survivors, a daughter of Chief Ninstints, provided Swanton with as many house names in 1900.

The southernmost group of Haida, who owned territories south of Lyell Island and had Ninstints as their main village, were known as the Kunghit Haida. Their remoteness had separated them linguistically from their northern neighbours, and Swanton claims that they had "considerable racial individuality. . . . were great fighters and sent expeditions in all directions" (1909:105).

Swanton suggests that the inhabitants of numerous small towns of the Kunghit Haida gathered at Ninstints in the middle decades of the nineteenth century. The family which ruled Ninstints at the time of first contact with the Europeans were Ravens, while an Eagle family controlled the village during the half century before it was abandoned.

Anthony Island is small and exposed to the sweep of the open Pacific. However, the village site of Ninstints is the most secluded and protected of all major Haida villages, since it lies in a sheltered bay on the eastern side of the island and is further protected by a rocky islet facing the village.

Facing page: **Poles associated with Houses 10 to 13. Fallen front plaques reveal burial chambers at the top of the mortuary poles.** *Newcombe,* 1901 (RBCM E83)

The main house row at Ninstints straddled a natural terrace bordering the bay. The northern end was bounded by a low marshy area, and the southern end opened onto a small meadow. The front row of the houses was broken by the incursion of the beach. The terrace may have been the preferred area for houses, but once the terrace sites had been occupied, expansion of the village resulted in a new row of houses, in front of the terrace, at the northern and southern ends of the village.

It is probable that *type 2* house construction originated at Ninstints. All the earlier houses were of this type, although some simpler structures replaced them late in the period of occupation. Three of the houses were known to have carved interior poles but no house pits.

Ninstints is the earliest recorded Haida town of the southern Queen Charlotte Islands. Ships' logs from the early sea otter trade provide many details about it and its inhabitants. Captain George Dixon mentioned the Kunghit Haida of Anthony Island in his journal for 24 July 1787, when eleven canoes came out to trade with his ship. By that time they were evidently already accustomed to the idea of trade with Europeans, since they showed no fear and brought skins to trade.

Robert Haswell in the log of the *Lady Washington,* commanded by Captain Robert Gray, for June 1789 reported that "a brisk trade was soon set on foot by Coya the chief, who bartered for all his subjects" (Howay

Panorama of the north end of Ninstints showing (from left) Houses 6 to 16.

1941:97). A visit by the same ship later in 1789, then commanded by Captain John Kendrick, witnessed growing tension between the Kunghit Haida and the white traders. When villagers stole the captain's laundry, which had been hung out to dry aboard ship, Kendrick ordered the two chiefs, Koyah and Skulkinanse, seized, and he held their lives against the return of his clothing. Although all but a few items were returned, Kendrick forced the chiefs to have all their remaining furs brought aboard and bought at a price he determined. The Ninstints people claim that Captain Kendrick:

> *Took Coyah, tied a rope around his neck, whipped him, painted his face, cut off his hair, took away from him a great many skins, and then turned him ashore. Coyah was now no longer a chief, but an "Ahliko," or one of the lower class.* (Howay 1925:287)

A few days after this incident, Kendrick returned to trade at Ninstints. The captain had been drinking and, without arming his crew, allowed at least fifty Haida on board to trade. Koyah seized the keys to the arms chests and forced the crew below decks for a short time, until Kendrick rallied and led his crew to regain their arms and clear the ship. Many natives were killed in the foray or by boat parties sent after them.

Newcombe **1901** (RBCM E76)

Koyah, in his desire for revenge, attempted to regain some of his former prestige by warring with other Haida villages. Captain Joseph Ingraham observed a party of twelve large canoes at Cumshewa Inlet heading towards Skidegate in August 1791. He was told that it was Koyah and Skulkinanse on their way to attack their old enemies, the Skidegate tribe. Undoubtedly other villages felt the scourge of his vengeance.

In 1794 Koyah succeeded in capturing two trading vessels, probably the American ship *Eleanora,* commanded by Simon Metcalfe, and a large British ship which was forced to put in near Ninstints to replace broken masts. The last attack was on the ship *Union* under Captain John Boit on 21 June 1795. Led by the head chief of the area, Scorch Eye or "Skoicheye," it was a disaster, resulting in the death of between fifty and seventy Haida with no loss to the sailors.

A heartbreaking smallpox epidemic beset the village in 1863. In December of that year, Francis Poole, who was mining at Skincuttle Inlet, noted in his narrative:

> At New Aberdeen we had compassionately taken a European on board as a passenger via Queen Charlotte to Victoria. As ill luck would have it what should he do but fall sick of small-pox, some days before we arrived at the coppermines? I entered a vehement protest against his being put on

shore, knowing only too well the certain consequences. The little skipper insisted, however, and then weighed anchor without him.

We whites, it is true, were not attacked (by smallpox); but scarce had the sick man landed when the Indians again caught it; and in a very short space of time some of our best friends of the Ninstence or Cape St. James tribe... had disappeared forever. (1872:194–5)

As with most Haida villages it is difficult to establish an exact date for the abandonment of Ninstints. Epidemics depopulated the village until by 1875 it was used only as a camp. Dawson states that it was deserted by the time of his visit in 1878. By 1884 when Chittenden visited there were thirty former inhabitants camped at the village.

Beginning in 1947, serious efforts were made to preserve some of the monuments from Ninstints. More than a dozen poles were shipped to museums in the south. In 1977 studies were launched to preserve the poles remaining on site. As a culmination of this effort, UNESCO in 1981 declared Ninstints to be "a World Heritage Site, of importance to the History of Mankind." *

* A more detailed history of Ninstints may be found in *Ninstints: Haida World Heritage Site* by George F. MacDonald (Vancouver: University of British Columbia Press 1983)

Above: **Members of the Ninstints Recovery Expedition at base of House 9 frontal pole. Several poles were carefully removed for display in museums. 1957** (B.C. Government)

Above left: **Five small, seated watchman figures were carved at the base of this mortuary for House 7.** *Barbeau,* **1947** (CMC 102780)

Below the mortuary plaque bearing the moon and thunderbird, an emblem of Koyah's people, is a crest showing a killer whale eating a man. *Newcombe, 1901* (RBCM E79).

North end of Ninstints. On the islet at right were shaman graves. *Newcombe, 1901* (RBCM E62)

Kaisun

KAISUN (SEA LION TOWN) LOCATED on Inskip Channel on the west coast of Moresby Island belonged to an Eagle lineage who settled there from their previous territory in Skidegate Inlet. Swanton claims that the townsite earlier belonged to a Raven lineage, who had abandoned it.

The village chief was named "Some costly things fall into his house." Europeans called him Skotsgai, a corruption of part of his name. They also frequently referred to the town as Gold Harbour, since it was near the gold strike at Mitchell Inlet, or as Old Gold Harbour, to differentiate it from New Gold Harbour (Haina).

John Work credits the town with eighteen houses and 329 people, while Swanton's informants remembered the names of twenty houses. Traces of only fifteen houses could be detected in mapping the village. Some of the names on Swanton's list may refer to houses built at different times on the same house sites. The town is clearly divided into moiety sections, with the Ravens to the west (Houses 1–8) and the Eagles to the east (Houses 9–15).

Skotsgai owned three houses in the village. His main house was probably House 10, since he cut off the top crest of the frontal pole of that house at the behest of an early missionary. The only mortuary in the village also stood in front of this house.

Kaisun was deserted by the mid-1870s.

Above: **Base of the frontal pole for House Upon Which Are Clouds, owned by Chief Skotsgai. The crest is a beaver. Note the frogs in its ears and the potlatch cylinders, records of feasts given by Skotsgai, above its head.** *Newcombe,* 1901 (RBCM E65)

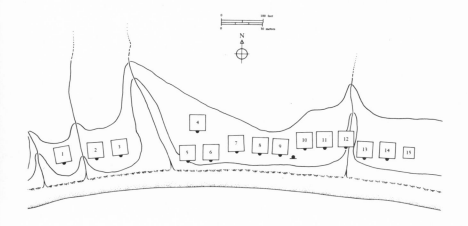

Facing page: **Thunderbird House (House 2) belonged to a chief named "Great supernatural power."** *Newcombe,* 1897 (RBCM E61)

Chaatl

CHAATL LIES ON A SIZEABLE ISLAND at the western end of Skidegate Inlet, facing south onto Buck Channel. At its western end, where the village is located, the channel is exposed to the open Pacific. A rough sea is frequent in front of the village, although the village itself is protected by rocky cliffs at its western end.

Swanton identifies Chaatl as the village of Kow-welth in John Work's list, assigned thirty-five houses with 561 inhabitants. Swanton's informants recalled the names of twenty-eight houses, not all of which were contemporary, but many more were said to have existed before a great fire destroyed a large part of the town sometime after 1878. Surveys in 1968 and 1970 found evidence of twenty-five house sites, as verified by photographs taken around the turn of the century.

Chaatl was settled by Raven and Eagle families from Pebble Town, a long abandoned village at Second Beach near Skidegate. They were joined by one Eagle family who originally lived at Skidegate but moved to Chaatl after one of them shot a Skidegate chief.

The head chief of the village was a Raven. The traditional name that accompanied the chieftainship was Nankilstlas, or "He whose voice is obeyed." In 1850 the reigning chief had the personal name Wadatstaia, but he was known to the whites as Captain Gold because he and his wife made the first gold find on the Islands.

The move from Chaatl to the eastern end of Skidegate Inlet, mostly to Haina, began shortly after 1859. It continued throughout the 1860s until Chaatl was virtually abandoned, although four or five simple plank houses were maintained until after the turn of the century. Captain Gold did not move to Haina but negotiated with Chief Skidegate for a house site at Second Beach.

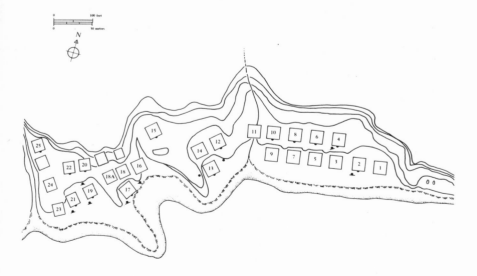

Facing page: **Chaatl from the eastern end in 1903. Although abandoned as a permanent settlement, some simple houses have been maintained for seasonal use.** Newcombe, 1903 (CFM 17691)

THE NORTHE

KAYANG

KIUSTA

RN VILLAGES : *MASSET*

...AN · HIELLAN · KUNG

...DADENS · YAKU · TIAN

MASSET

THE VILLAGE OF MASSET STANDS just inside Masset Inlet on the eastern shore. Its Haida name was Uttewas, which means "White Slope" in the Masset dialect, likely referring to a tall hill at the southern end of the village that has quantities of clam shells, remains of ancient meals, eroding from its banks. The hill itself is called Idjao, a name also used for a collection of houses south of the hill. Uttewas and Idjao amalgamated as a single village in the latter half of the nineteenth century.

The first explorer to enter Masset Inlet and leave a description of Uttewas village was Lieutenant Camille de Roquefeuil, in September 1817:

> *We passed the southeast point, and soon after, being opposite to a large village, we were surrounded by canoes. . . . As far as we could judge, the huts composing the four villages on the two sides of the entrance are better built, and in better order, than those to the north. There is something picturesque in the whole appearance of this large village. It is particularly remarkable for the monstrous and colossal figures which decorate the houses of the principal inhabitants, the wide gaping mouths of which serve as a door. . . . (1823:87–8)*

Extensive change met mineral surveyor Newton Chittenden, who visited Masset inlet in 1884:

> *There are three villages near the entrance to Masset Inlet. Yan—abandoned—with 20 houses and 25 carved poles, on the west side, and Ut-te-was,—now Masset—and Kayung, situated about a mile below, on the east. Masset is the principal village of the Haida nation, now containing a population of about three hundred and fifty Indians, 40 occupied houses, 50 carved poles, and the ruins of many ancient lodges. (1884:23)*

The maximum population figures that can be justified for Masset on the basis of the site plan and early photographs, which document thirty-two houses, would be 1,280 people. This figure includes both Uttewas and Idjao villages around 1860–70. John Work estimates that between 1836 and 1841 there were more than twice this number. He may have included the

Facing page: **Between the house posts from Grizzly Bear House (House 10) are displayed a Chilkat blanket and a painted woven hat. On the wall are ceremonial daggers. This display is typical of one made at the funeral of a chief.** *Maynard,* **1884** (CMC)

Several variations of the memorial pole show in this photograph of Monster House (House 13). All display rings that mark potlatches. *Dossetter 1881* (RBCM 33607)

other Masset Inlet villages of Yan and Kayang in his estimate of 2,473 people. Even so, his figure, if accurate, gives a telling indication of the scale of the population loss which took place over just a few decades.

The map depicts the village of Masset in 1880. There is direct evidence for all the thirty-seven houses of traditional style which stood there at that time. Only ten houses have the *type 2* frame, although these included the largest houses in the village.

The town chieftainship of Masset originally rested with a Raven lineage. The names Sigai ("The open sea") and Xa'na alternated as chiefs' names. In the 1840s Chief Sigai decided before his death to pass the chieftainship of the town to his own son, Wiah, an Eagle, rather than to his eldest sister's eldest son, as dictated by tradition. Protest arose, but Sigai persisted, saying: "I got a son and he became wealthy by his own right: I do not want him to be a common member of the village, so I gave him this village" (Blackman 1972:212). The resulting split remains in Masset to this day.

The new chief, Wiah, provided strong leadership for the village. In 1852, at his direction, the crew of the disabled ship *Susan Sturges* were kept as slaves until ransomed by the Hudson's Bay Company. Wiah's dominance was manifest in the huge dwelling called Monster House (House 13), which he erected near the centre of the village. A year before his death in 1883, Wiah was one of the first Haida to be baptized a Christian.

The last quarter of the nineteenth century witnessed a drastic decline in the population of Masset despite the influx of Haida from more remote villages on the north coast of Graham Island, which were abandoned totally in this period. The turmoil of mixing together the chiefs of families that were formerly fiercely independent is epitomized by the actions of Chief Edenshaw, who moved into Masset in the early 1870s. In front of a fine totem pole which had belonged to his ancestors he:

> Danced a most strange and beautiful dance for about a quarter of an hour, and at its conclusion ordered the totem to be cast upon the fire and burnt, so that no other chief would ever be able to dance as he had done before this totem for a bygone ancestor. (Harrison 1925:168)

In this way he signified his submission to Chief Wiah.

With the arrival in 1873 of the first missionary, William H. Collison, a process began which saw all the traditional houses and poles disappear within a quarter century. The missionaries demanded that poles be torn down and destroyed, and communal dwellings abandoned in favour of European-style houses.

Inhabitants of Monster House pose with a visiting government official. The ceremonial boardwalk, stretching to the beach, can be seen in the foreground. *Dossetter* 1881 (CMC)

Dr. Kude, a famous shaman of Masset, stands second from left. Xa'na, a Masset chief, stands at right. Note the tattoos on his chest and arms. The other two figures are masked shamans. *Dossetter, 1881* (AMNH 42314)

Edenshaw House (House 7) showing the use of European building materials in traditional dwellings. (CMC 520962)

Star House with its inhabitants. *Reford* (NMC 71-4371)

KAYANG

Little has been recorded about Kayang. Perhaps it was overshadowed by Masset, located farther north on the east shore of Masset Inlet. In 1884 Richard Maynard first photographed the village with a panoramic view from the south end. Less than half the houses appear to have been occupied at that time.

At least ten well-carved poles are documented for Kayang. The style of carving is virtually identical to that found at Masset.

The village is a classic example of the moiety organization of a Haida village. The first five houses from the south end of town belonged to Eagles, while eight of the nine houses in the north end belonged to Ravens.

The site survey indicated that there were more prepared house floors than there were houses in Swanton's list. Although these sites are shown on the map, it is almost certain that houses were never built on them, since Swanton's list corresponds with the photographs. The village probably was never completed to the extent planned because of population decline.

There appear to have been only two *type 2* houses at Kayang, with the *type 1* style in the majority, as at Masset. European-style houses replaced the old plank houses in the last two decades of the nineteenth century. One of the old posts of a double mortuary still stands between the paved highway and the beach a few miles south of Masset, marking the old location of Kayang. The name itself has disappeared from official signs but is still recognized by the older Haida who live there.

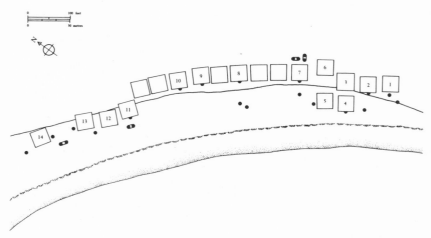

Above: **Model of House 7 (c1898) with embellishment of gable painting and carved house posts.** (BM)

Facing page: **Goose House (House 7) was the most frequently photographed house in Kayang, no doubt because it had the most elaborate frontal pole, now in the Museum of Mankind in London, England.** *Maynard, 1888* (CFM 17459)

Yan is situated in a sheltered cove on the west shore at the mouth of Masset Inlet, only a few miles from Masset. In the Haida language Yan means "directly opposite a ledge." According to Swanton the village was built in relatively recent times, about the end of the eighteenth century, following a dispute between two Masset families, one of which moved to Yan. Other related Raven families joined them there, establishing some thirteen houses. They were joined, in time, by two related Eagle families from the nearby villages of Widja and Totlka and another from Tcets, who established another seven houses between them.

The village was divided between Houses 8 and 9, with the Ravens to the south and the Eagles to the north. The two exceptions are Houses 14 and 15, which belonged to Ravens but are in the Eagle part of town.

Yan appeared to be thriving during Dossetter's visit in 1881, but within the decade the entire population abandoned it and resettled at Masset. For some reason, perhaps its proximity to the dominant village of Masset that attracted the attention of the early traders and missionaries, Yan was not visited often, and few written accounts of it survive.

Above: **Villagers gathered in front of a memorial for Ildjiwas, owner of Flicker House (House 12).** *Dossetter, 1881* (CMC VII-B-69)

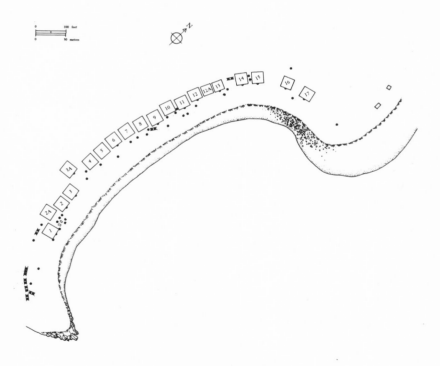

Facing page: **View of Yan from House 1 looking north.** *Newcombe 1913* (RBCM E617)

Below: **An unusual multiple mortuary on three posts south of Yan held three coffins. It bore an elaborate crest carving of a thunderbird on its front plaque.** *Newcombe, 1913* (CMC J-209643)

Left: **Yan village from the south in 1881. Carved ravens graced the corner posts of Killer Whale House (House 1) (left).** *Dossetter, 1881* (AMNH 42296)

HIELLAN, ANGLICIZED FROM ITS HAIDA NAME TLIELANG, stood on the east bank of the Hiellan River, near its mouth, on the northeast coast of Graham Island. On the opposite bank is Tow Hill, a prominent volcanic cone remnant that provided a landmark for canoes crossing Dixon Entrance. Dawson notes that:

> *A few much decayed carved posts and beams of former houses are still standing where, according to the Indians, a large village formerly existed. Its disappearance is partly accounted for by the fact that the sea has washed away much of the ground on which it stood.* (1880:164B)

The village undoubtedly was occupied over a long period of the prehistoric past, since there are two branches of Eagles which trace their origin to Hiellan. The most important Eagle chief at Hiellan was Sqilao, who owned the largest house in the village but was not the town chief. That honour belonged to Giatlins, chief of a Raven lineage with whom the Eagles shared the village.

The location of Hiellan is excellent from both an economic and a defensive point of view. The Hiellan River, which forms one boundary of the site, is rich in salmon runs, while razor clams and other shellfish abound on the extensive tidal flats which form the other boundary.

The steep sides of Tow Hill provided a defensive advantage to Hiellan. The Tsimshian war narratives collected by Barbeau describe an elaborate fort on the hill, with the palisades set at overhanging angles. Entry was gained through a trap door angled forward to make it heavy and difficult to open from the outside.

Swanton describes a war party of Ravens from Hiellan that, in about 1860, attacked the Nishga near the latter's village of Anguidah on the Nass River. The attackers were successful and, singing songs of victory, brought slaves back to Hiellan. A short while later, the people of Hiellan feared reprisals and took refuge in Masset. When the Nishga finally did mount a retaliatory raid, they found Hiellan deserted and burned it to the ground. The Hiellan people saw the smoke from the destruction all the way from Masset and launched a counterattack. The battle lasted the whole day, with many casualties on both sides.

The Raven families seem to have moved permanently to Masset after this episode. Various Eagle lineages had relocated to Kiusta already. A small community based on clam and fish canning sprang up on the site during the 1920s, destroying what remained of the old village. Since the 1930s, the cannery has been abandoned.

Charles Edenshaw claimed that seven houses stood at the village, but Swanton recorded the names of only three. The remains of five houses were located during the National Museums of Canada site survey in 1981.

Above: **Detail from the frontal pole of House For a Large Crowd of People (House 1), notable for its many small crest figures.** (UCA)

Facing page: **Frontal pole of House For a Large Crowd of People** (CMC 46694)

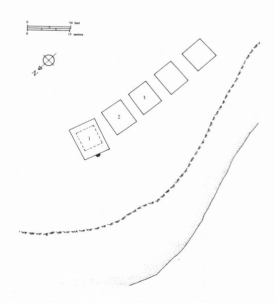

KUNG

KUNG IS IN A WELL PROTECTED LOCATION inside the narrows on the east shore of Virago Sound. A small stream bounds the southern end of the village site. From the ground plan of the village, which provides evidence of a triple row of houses, as well as from the photographs, which show ancient and decayed mortuaries, it appears that there had been an earlier village on this site prior to its occupation in the latter half of the nineteenth century. John Work uses the name Nightasis for this earlier village and reports that about 1840 it had fifteen houses with 280 inhabitants.

The early village probably was continuously occupied until a major influx of Eagles occurred in 1853. With the gradual abandonment of Kiusta village, Chief Albert Edward Edenshaw resettled with his followers at Kung. Dawson, who visited the village in 1878, writes that:

> It has been a substantial and well-constructed (village), but is now rather decayed, though some of the houses are still inhabited. The houses arranged along the edge of a low bank, facing a fine sandy beach, are eight to ten in number, some of them quite large. The carved posts are not numerous, though in a few instances elaborate. (1880:163B)

Shortly after Dawson's visit, Kung itself was abandoned in the general movement to the larger villages.

Swanton questioned elderly people in Masset in 1899 and recorded the names and owners of twelve houses, but this list is probably only accurate for the village in its last stage of occupation.

In effect, the western and eastern segments of the house row originally formed separate, small, two-rowed hamlets. However, from the photographs it appears that the two rows were occupied alternately. That is, the house sites behind Houses 1 to 4 were the earliest inhabited, perhaps before the mid-nineteenth century. They were relatively simple structures, with no evidence of carved frontal or interior poles. They probably belonged to Eagles, as did the houses directly in front which replaced them. These newer houses belonged to the families who accompanied Edenshaw from Kiusta.

The style of the posts at Kung is distinctive, with strong cross-ties to those of the Kaigani Haida. One feature of this style is a rib-like design inside the ear space of large crest figures, such as bears and sea grizzlies. Another is the large diameter of the cylinders that emerge from the top of the house frontal poles. Neither of these traits is common on the Queen Charlotte Islands.

Facing page: **The intricate carving of these memorial poles is characteristic of Kung style.** *Curtis,* 1914 (EAG)

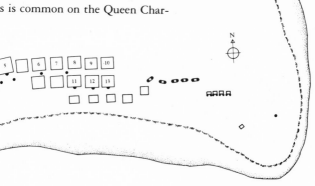

The figure on the right post of this shaman mortuary is a shaman holding his rattle. His face is surrounded by a monstrous figure that represents his spirit familiar and helper. *Dorsey, 1897* (CFM 2633)

This roughly built house at Yatze was never replaced by a more permanent structure. *Newcombe, 1913* (AMNH 106694)

KIUSTA LIES ON A SHELTERED BEACH facing Cloak Bay on the northwest corner of Graham Island, opposite Langara Island. To the north is Parry Passage, noted for its tidal currents, but the village is well protected by Marchand Reef. The name of the town means "Where the trail comes out," in reference to a substantial trail that is still used between this village and Lepas Bay on the west coast of Graham Island.

Abundant sea otter around Langara Island brought many traders to the area in the last two decades of the eighteenth century, but few mentioned Kiusta in their journals.

The first reference to the village was made by John Meares in the journal of the expedition of the *Iphigenia,* under Captain William Douglas:

> *At five o'clock (on 20 June 1789) they dropped the bower anchor in twenty-five fathoms of water, about four miles from the shore, and two from a small, barren, rocky island, which happened to prove the residence of a chief, named Blakaw Coneehaw, whom Douglas had seen on the coast in his last voyage. He came immediately on board, and welcomed the arrival of the ship with a song, to which two hundred of his people formed a chorus of the most pleasing melody. When the voices ceased, he paid Captain Douglas the compliment of exchanging names with him.* (Meares 1790:367)

The "Coneehaw" (or "Cunneaw") referred to was Chief Gunia, an Eagle chief who lived in a house on a small island near Kiusta, from which he exerted influence over villages in the area. The town chief of Kiusta was Itltini, also an Eagle. Near the end of the eighteenth century Gunia moved with his lineage to the Prince of Wales Archipelago in southeast Alaska.

It is not clear what links existed between Chief Gunia and his successor, Chief Edenshaw. The name of Douglas that Gunia received was passed on to Edenshaw, which led Albert Edward Edenshaw, who succeeded his uncle about 1850, to claim a special relationship with Governor James Douglas. By the time of Dawson's visit to the village site in 1878, it was so overgrown with brush that he did not bother to photograph it, although he notes in his journal:

> *It is difficult to imagine on what account the village has been abandoned unless from sheer lack of inhabitants, as it seems admirably suited for the purpose of the Haida.*

By 1853 the population of Kiusta had declined seriously, and the occupants followed their chief, Edenshaw, east to Kung. An extensive archaeological project conducted at the village in 1972 indicated that there were at least fourteen house sites and thirty-one poles, including frontal poles, memorials, and mortuaries. There were several isolated houses at the far northwest end of the village, near some mortuary posts. The survey also turned up much evidence of argillite carving at Kiusta. Many early argillite panel pipes attributed to the Edenshaws may have been carved there.

Above: **Model of Story House (House 7).** (AMNH 36150)

Facing page: **This multiple-post mortuary shows the crests shared by all the families in Kiusta: the beaver, raven, frog, eagle, black whale, and supernatural whale. It may be the mortuary for the first Edenshaw to settle at Kiusta. 1952** (RBCM)

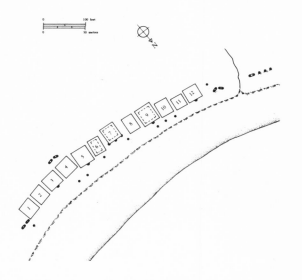

DADENS

DADENS IS ON THE SOUTH COAST of Langara Island, facing Lucy Island in Parry Passage. At the time of the first recorded contact with Europeans in 1789 the village was owned by a Raven lineage. Although the head chief of this lineage was named Nanadjigias ("One unable to buy"), the town chief of Dadens was Gao, called Cow or Kow by the early European traders and explorers who frequently visited and described the village in the late eighteenth century. In 1789 the village contained substantial houses and several carved poles, and even boasted potato patches, indicating to Captain William Douglas and his crew that they were not the first to visit the area. A fire swept Dadens shortly after Douglas's visit. Rather than rebuild, the inhabitants emigrated to Alaska and settled Klinkwan and other villages.

The village fire may have provided a convenient rationale for the move to Alaska, but other factors played a part. Throughout the coastal area at this time there was constant jockeying among the chiefs of lineages for the best position relative to the Europeans. Many chiefs may have thought it better to move closer to the new Russian trading post at Sitka, where a year-round supply of goods was assured. Since Haida lineages were autonomous groups, they had no special loyalty to any one village.

The move to Alaska was probably a piecemeal affair spanning many years. Dawson and Swanton both thought that the evidence they collected form informants pointed to a move north about 1720, which led Swanton to puzzle over Douglas's 1789 report of a sizeable permanent village. It is possible that the movement of Ravens to Alaska took place in several waves, the first in the early 1700s and a later one in the 1790s.

Dadens' early historical record is particularly rich. One 1791 visitor was Captain Joseph Ingraham from Boston, master of the brigantine *Hope*:

> *After the vessel was fast I went in the boat accompanied by Cow (Gao) to view two pillars which were situated in the front of a village about a quarter of a mile distant from our vessel on the north shore. They were about 40 feet in height, carved in a very curious manner indeed representing men, toads, etc., the whole of which I tho't did great credit to the natural genius of these people. In one of the houses of this village the door was through the mouth of one of the before-mentioned images. In another was a large square pit with seats all round it sufficient to contain a great number of people.* (n.d.)

Captain Chanal and Surgeon Roblet, who visited the village in the early 1790s, observed that the people of Dadens had a surfeit of English trade items and wanted only guns and powder. Their account indicated the extent to which the Haida used European trade goods:

> *Here are seen confounded with wooden vessels and spoons of horn or whalebone, peculiar to the country, iron pots and kettles, stew-pans, frying pans, tin basins, and other household utensils, which the Europeans have furnished the Americans, and the use of which is become as familiar to them as to ourselves.* (Fleurieu 1801:419–20)

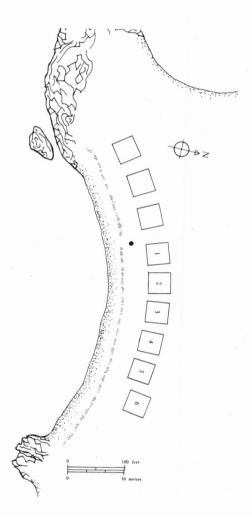

Facing page: **The only pole standing at Dadens in the late nineteenth century.** *Dawson, 1878* (NAC 268)

YAKU

ONE AND A HALF MILES EAST OF KIUSTA on the other side of Marchand Reef stood the village of Yaku, facing east into Parry Passage from a well-protected beach. In early accounts it was frequently grouped with Kiusta, as in Work's designation of the two towns as Lu-lan-na, with a total of 296 people inhabiting twenty houses. In 1900, Swanton's informants recalled four large houses and four small ones. On this basis Swanton attributed to it a population of 100 to 120 people. Yaku belonged to Ravens, of whom the chief was Xi.

Kiusta was the only Haida village that was fortified by a surrounding ditch and palisade. Swan described this feature in 1883:

> *An ancient moat surrounds (the) village enclosing about 8 acres. Edenshaw said it was ancient and for defence purposes. . . . (It) extends in a semicircle from the sea, draining a swamp. Dirt from it was pulled up on (the) inside forming a bank at least 15 feet from (the) bottom of (the) ditch. On top was a stockade and split trees.*

The National Museums of Canada survey in 1966 found clear evidence of the fortifications preserved behind the village. Remains of four houses were found, including house timbers, two frontal poles, and two house depressions. A cleared area on either side could have accommodated several additional houses.

Facing page: **Coastal vegetation had reclaimed Yaku by the turn of the century.** *Newcombe,* 1913 (RBCM E626)

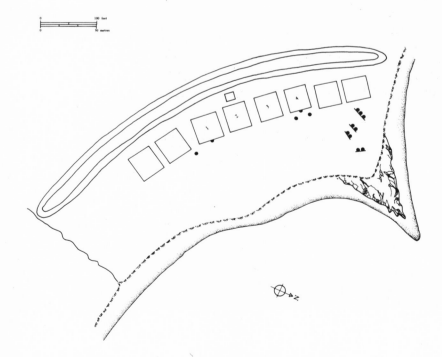

TIAN

TIAN OR SLAUGHTER VILLAGE lies on a beach facing southeast into a bay on the west coast of Graham Island. Offshore are numerous rocky islands where migrating sea lions haul out, which may account for the name of the village. The village belonged to the same Raven lineage which owned Yaku. Its chief was "Wet island."

Tian is probably the village John Work called "Too." In 1846 he ascribed to it ten houses and 196 inhabitants. Only seven houses could be clearly distinguished in 1968.

The village is well hidden from ships sailing up the coast and was never visited by the early explorers. It was abandoned in the 1850s, before any house names could be recorded or photographs taken.

Although corner posts and roof timbers are relatively well preserved, the only identifiable house site is at the west end of the house row. It was larger and better constructed than the rest and has an excavated house pit. The gable of this house, as well as those of other houses, is extremely low. Were it not for the house pit, a person could not stand except in the centre of the house.

None of the houses had frontal poles, and the adzing on the corner posts was extremely rough. Some of the preserved carving has a peculiarly archaic appearance.

Facing page: **One of eight elaborate double-post mortuaries scattered throughout the village. c1920** (CMC J-20026-5)

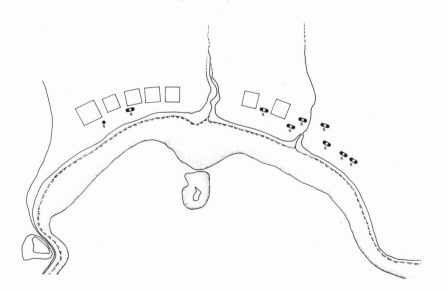

House interior post, Skidegate (AMNH 42288)

SELECTED REFERENCES

BLACKMAN, MARGARET B. 1972 *Nei:w)ns,* the "monster" house of Chief *Wi:ha*: An exercise in ethnohistorical, archaeological, and ethnological reasoning. *Syesis* 5:211–15

CHITTENDEN, NEWTON 1884 *Exploration of the Queen Charlotte Islands.* Victoria

COLLISON, WILLIAM H. 1915 *In the Wake of the War Canoe.* London: Seeley, Service (rpt. Victoria: Sono Nis 1981)

DAWSON, GEORGE M. 1880 Report on the Queen Charlotte Islands. Geological Survey of Canada, *Report on Progress for 1878–79*

DIXON, GEORGE 1789 *A Voyage Round the World; but More Particularly to the Northwest Coast of America . . . in the "King George" and "Queen Charlotte."* London

FLEURIEU, CHARLES PIERRE CLARET DE 1801 *A Voyage Round the World, Performed during the Years 1790, 1791, 1792, by Etienne Marchand. . . .* London

HARRISON, CHARLES 1925 *Ancient Warriors of the North Pacific.* London: Witherby

HOWAY, F.W. 1920 The Voyage of the *Hope. Washington Historical Quarterly* 11:3–28. 1925 Indian Attacks upon Maritime Traders of the Northwest Coast, 1785–1805. *Canadian Historical Review* 6:287–309

INGRAHAM, JOSEPH n.d. Journal of the Voyage of the Brigantine *Hope* from Boston to the Northwest Coast of North America. Manuscript in Library of Congress (DV 620.H44#3). Washington, DC

MACDONALD, GEORGE F. 1983a *Haida Monumental Art: Villages of the Queen Charlotte Islands.* Vancouver: University of British Columbia Press. 1983b *Ninstints: Haida World Heritage Site.* Vancouver: University of British Columbia Press

MEARES, JOHN 1790 *Voyages Made in the Years 1788 and 1789 from China to the Northwest Coast of America . . . in the Ship "Nootka". . . .* London

POOLE, FRANCIS 1872 *Queen Charlotte Islands: A Narrative of Discovery and Adventure in the North Pacific.* London

ROQUEFEUIL, M. CAMILLE DE 1823 *A Voyage Round the World Between the Years 1816–1819 in the Ship "Le Bordelais."* London. Trans. by C.P.C. de Fleurieu. London

SWAN, JAMES G. n.d. Journal of a trip to Queen Charlotte Islands, B.C. (1883). Microfilm. University of Washington Library, Seattle

SWANTON, JOHN R. 1909 Contribution to the Ethnology of the Haida. American Museum of Natural History *Memoirs* 8:1–300